The Angels Told
Me

Mary B. Frances

&

A. Z. Love

Angel Spirit Books

All Rights Reserved

Copyright © 2021

Mary B. Frances

A. Z. Love

This book is based on true events that have taken place in Mary B. Frances' life. All characters within are actual persons or Spirits. Characters, places, and incidents have been recalled to the best of the author's ability. The names of some individuals have changed to respect their privacy. The author recognizes that other people's memory of happened events may differ from the author's.

Design, Layout, and Editing:

Co Press Publishing, LLC

Hardback ISBN 978-0-578-31866-0
Ebook   ISBN 978-0-578-31865-3

All rights reserved. No part of this document may be reproduced or transmitted in any form or by any means, electronic, mechanical, photocopying, recording, or otherwise, without prior written permission of the publisher or authors, except by a reviewer who may quote brief passages for articles or reviews. For information: email AngelSpiritBooks@yahoo.com

This book is dedicated to all people in the sincere hope that through prayer and faith, you too will know the Angel Spirit within ...

Power of Prayer

Are miracles only those that we see
Where do they come from, what could it be
Which brings about such miraculous change
That can ease suffering and much pain

Yes, everyone should be aware
That there is nothing as powerful
As the power of prayer

To kneel down on bended knees
Is one action that will surely please
The one who needs to be pleased the most
The All-knowing and Almighty host

And all those times you feel real low
Not knowing which way to go
You must always, always be aware
That there is nothing as powerful
As the power of prayer

But first, you must do your part
And the first place that you can start
When things don't work out the first time
Never give up, always keep trying

Keep the faith and do what you can
And when that doesn't work, just try again

But this time, try a different way
See what happens when you pray
Every night and every day
And always, always be aware
That there is nothing as powerful as
The power of prayer
— **Journey of Thoughts, 1997**

Foreword

I met Mary B. Frances on the telephone. She was introduced to me through her brother, Johnnie (Thomas), a friend of mine. Her brother always spoke of her, but she was the sister who lived out of state.

We talked for hours during that first phone call. I mean literally from about four in the morning until around two thirty in the afternoon. Mostly, we spoke of events and things that happened in our lives where our Spirits guided and uplifted us.

Mary did most of the talking. Once she started, she was boundless. We continued talking for days. Mary had many things to talk about. Although sometimes, the stories were the same and just got repeated. Nevertheless, the stories were absorbing and intriguing.

Mary expressed her interest in wanting to write a book. I imagined a book about the many captivating things that Mary speaks about would be most enthralling to read. We then conspired to write ***The Angels Told Me***.

Thank you, Mary B. Frances, for the opportunity to conspire with you. Thank you for believing in Angels.

A. Z. Love

Preface

I wrote this book because; I want to share some of my life experiences. I want to let others know that the power of prayer can be a great weapon. There have been a lot of unusual things that have happened to me. I was often picked on as a child because I was different.

You see, I was born veiled-birth, and sometimes I see things that other people do not. Some folks have never heard of such a thing, but some folks have. Those who have heard of babies born with a veil know what I'm speaking of. I can see Spirits, and I can sometimes see death too. There are people alive today who can testify to some of the things I talk about in this book.

Other people might fear me, or get angry at me, because I may know certain things before they do. Is it my fault that I was born this way? Once, when I was a child, I pushed this little boy on the side of his head, and the white Angel Girl ran up and punched me on the side of my head. Oh yeah, that's in the book too!

So, buckle up, and hold on tight. Try to hang on with all your might. You are about to take a ride on a real-life journey. Now, turn the page, and see what The Angels Told Me.

CONTENTS

Cousin Sally and Cousin Buddy .- 1 -
The Ride to Hell ....- 12 -
The Rotten Shack ....- 17 -
The Dog Angel ....- 25 -
The Beating ....- 36 -
The Devil and the Water ....- 47 -
The Two Escapes ....- 54 -
The Angel in the Car ....- 60 -
The Rescue ....- 68 -
Momma Daisy ....- 75 -
The Dog Pan ....- 83 -
The Ball in the Ditch ....- 95 -
The Gold Coins ....- 105 -
The Baron ....- 110 -
The Trained Chickens ....- 118 -
The White Angel Girl ....- 124 -
The Bus That Crashed ....- 131 -
The Miracle Oil ....- 149 -
The Knock on the Door ....- 157 -
The Sun Healed Me ....- 163 -
Sandra and the Touch ....- 168 -
The Man at Penn Station ....- 175 -

A War is Coming	- 183 -
The Pandemic	- 194 -
The Pandemic Surges	- 206 -
Contact	- 221 -
References	- 222 -
Acknowledgments	- 223 -
Angel Spirit Books	- 224 -
What Kind of Prayers	- 225 -
About the Author	- 226 -

COUSIN SALLY AND COUSIN BUDDY

I'm remembering when I am a young girl. It was around the year 1953. I am living in Jacksonville, Florida with my Momma and my two brothers. I am around eight years old. I'm a skinny, caramel skin girl with long, fluffy, curly hair. Folks say that Thomas and I have hair like our Mother's, and I have dimples and a smile like my Father's.

Thomas is the youngest sibling. He is five years younger than me, so that would make him three. My brother Oliver is seven and his hair is thicker than Thomas' and mine. His skin tone is much lighter, like a brown paper bag. Oliver is quiet and doesn't like to play a lot.

One hot summer day, my brother Thomas and I are playing in the bedroom of our tiny, dull, two rooms apartment.

Our apartment is on the first floor. Momma made the biggest room in the apartment the bedroom. We do everything in the bedroom. You may as well say we live in that room. It's the only room in the house that has a door. That is a door that leads to the outside.

We all sleep in that dimly lit room. Momma sleeps on the only bed in the house. It's a regular-size bed with a dingy-looking mattress on top of a lopsided box spring. On top of Momma's bed is a military blanket.

We have plenty of military blankets. I guess that's a good thing because the left over blankets sometimes become pallets. We children slept on pallets that we made on the floor.

… They're not at all like the bed pallets of today. …

Our pallets are made of pillow cases stuffed with clothing, old rags, blankets, you name it. It's made from anything soft like that you can sleep on. In the summer time, sleeping on pallets on the floor is not so bad, but in the winter time, the floor can get really cold. I mean really cold!

The second room is so small. I don't know if it can even be called a room because it does not have a door to it. It looks about as big as a love seat.

There is a small coffee table in the tiny room with a hot plate used for cooking on it and piled high with whatever else we can fit on that table.

I was just about to tag Thomas and yell, "You're it," when someone began knocking on the door.

I heard Momma saying, "Who is it?"

"It's me, Cousin Sally," the voice replies on the other side of the door.

Momma quickly opens the door and let Cousin Sally in. Cousin Sally came waltzing into our bedroom and then suddenly stops short.

She looks at me and my brother Thomas and says, "Ooh Daisy," talking to Momma. "You should let me take these two pretty little curly head babies with me," and began to ruffle our hair with her rough, looking hands.

… Come to think of it, I never did like people touching my hair. …

Momma immediately looks at us and asks, "Do ya'll want to go home with Cousin Sally?"

Me and Thomas look at each other with wide eyes. Now Cousin Sally is Momma's first cousin. She and her husband, Cousin Buddy, live somewhere near Macon, Georgia. They had taken

Oliver with them to Georgia last month. He stayed with them for about a week. Oliver said that he had fun while at Cousin Sally's house. I remember hearing him say that, "She was good to me."

We both reply quickly, "Yes, we want to go!"

Momma then turns and looks at Cousin Sally. Momma don't have to turn her head much because it looks like the room has gotten even smaller after Cousin Sally came in.

Momma asks, "When you bringing them back?"

"Next week," Cousin Sally replies.

Next, Momma took a large brown paper bag and put me one dress and one pair of underwear that she had made for me in it. She then put a pair of short pants and a short sleeve shirt in the bag for Thomas. She didn't put any underwear in the bag for Thomas. We didn't have much, and the weather was still so hot. Now that we are all packed and ready to go, Momma hands me the paper bag.

"Ya'll be good now," she says reaching out her arms, hugging both of us.

When we went outside, I can see Cousin Buddy sitting on the driver's side in an old white looking two-seater car. It don't look like we would fit in his small car. It was an old model car that we soon learn had to be hand cranked to start.

… It was definitely an antique and today it would be worth a whole lot of money. …

As I was wondering where us kids would sit, Cousin Buddy jumps out of the car and opens what may have been the trunk. He then removes some things from this small compartment and motions with his hand and said with a big grin.

"Come on ya'll, and get in the buddy seat."

He lifts me up and put me in the buddy seat. Afterwards, he lifts Thomas up and put him next to me and said, "Ya'll be alright. Just don't move around and you won't fall out." And that's where we sat for the entire ride.

Cousin Buddy smiles and walks to the front of the car. He bends down and turns this rusty looking knob sticking out from the front of the car. After turning that rusty looking knob around and then around again, the car starts and Cousin Buddy got back into the driver's seat.

We all wave and shout goodbye to Momma and Oliver as they stood in the window of our small two room apartment waving goodbye.

I sure hope that I don't miss Momma too much. I have never been away from home before.

THE RIDE TO HELL

Boy did we have fun as we rode to Georgia. It's very hot today, but Thomas and I have a nice breeze going on sitting in the buddy seat. It's like sitting smack dab in front of a fan. Our curly hair was blowing all in our faces and, we're just laughing and enjoying ourselves when Cousin Sally shouts from inside the car in a cold mean voice that made me shiver.

"Ya'll kids stop moving around so d--n much before you fall out. Can't have you hurting yourselves before the crops get ripe, now can we."

I never heard Cousin Sally swear before and I don't know what crops she is talking about, so I quickly reply, "No Mam. We won't fall out."

My brother and I still was having fun with the wind blowing through our hair. We are happy. We just don't move around as much so we won't fall out of the buddy seat. Down the road we went.

We never thought this would be the ride to hell.

The first stop we made is at this big white house. I thought maybe that this is where Cousin Sally and Cousin Buddy live but it's not.

When the car stops, Cousin Buddy picks up Thomas first and then lifts me out of the buddy seat. It feels good to finally stand up straight, I thought as I stretch my arms high above my head. By this time Cousin Sally had made it out of the car.

"Ya'll stay out here and play. We'll be back in a few minutes." she said smoothing out the wrinkles in her skirt.

Cousin Sally and Uncle Buddy went into the house through the back door. We stay in the backyard and play and play. A few minutes turned into about an hour or so.

Finally, Cousin Sally and Cousin Buddy came back outside. We are so glad to see them because it is beginning to get a little dark outside.

Cousin Buddy puts us back into the buddy seat. As we are leaving, I notice an old woman standing in the back door looking in our direction. There is also an old man who was standing in the yard by the door. I guess they must live in the white house, I thought, as we drove away.

I wonder if they are Cousin Sally or Cousin Buddy's parents. Maybe they are just neighbors or people that they know. I sure will be glad to get to our destination.

THE ROTTEN SHACK

We drove for about five or ten minutes down this dirt road before eventually pulling in front of a rotten looking shack. There was no paint on the shack and it looks scary from down here. The shack was way up on a hill and the road was way down below like going through a valley.

We all got out of the car and began walking up the ragged, steep steps to the porch. It was a lot of tattered looking steps leading to the shack. As we got closer to the shack, I can tell that it had not been painted. I tightly held on to Thomas' hand so he wouldn't fall through the cracks in the steps all while clutching the brown paper bag that Momma had packed for us.

Once we got on the porch, Cousin Sally said, "Ya'll wait outside."

Cousin Sally and Cousin Buddy went inside the shack. We wait outside like we were told to. After a while we began wondering what was taking so long.

"I sure hope they come get us," I finally said. It's turning into dusk out here and I'm hungry.

"I want something to eat too," chimed Thomas sounding very much like a baby. After all he is only three years old.

I sure wish Momma had packed us some lunch in our brown paper bag, I thought as my stomach starts growling. I began wondering what Momma and Oliver were doing.

Eventually, Cousin Sally and Cousin Buddy came to the door that didn't have a door. They looked out of the doorway and said, "Ya'll come on in now."

We enter the shack not knowing what to expect. After all, the house doesn't even have a front door. It has a large worn looking trunk that is being used as a door.

Thomas and I began to walk through the shack while Cousin Sally and Cousin Buddy are in the bedroom. We go into the kitchen. There is a wood burning stove located on the left side of the doorway entering the kitchen. I sure wish there was some food on it, I thought as my stomach growls again.

Next we went to the back door. Although I am only eight years old, this door looks rotten to me. It was barely a door at all with pieces of wood missing and the door knob half dangling from its socket. We manage to open the door and walk to the very top step. There are just as many steps in the back of the house as it is in the front.

When I look across the field, I see nothing but lots of land and cotton. Lots and lots of cotton as far as my eyes can see. Thomas and I walk back into the kitchen and stood looking out of the window.

By now Cousin Sally had come into the kitchen. She pulls up the only chair in the house and sat by the window next to us. I want to run and hide. I was so scared of her.

That's when I said, "Ooh, all of this pretty cotton. I like picking cotton."

I don't know why I said that, I thought as I stood nervously looking out of the window. Cotton is soft and pretty, but I always get stuck by thorns when picking cotton. I want to move away from the window, but I was scared to move. I was always taught to respect adults, and I just want to please Cousin Sally.

Cousin Sally seem like she has changed since she knocked on Momma's door. She was like Jekyll and Hyde and before long she blurted out.

"Good you like picking it, cause you gonna' get it. You gonna' get it," she said again referring to the cotton.

I was scared by the tone of her voice. I mean really scared. Her voice went from a soft tone to a harsh mean tone voice. I look at Thomas and Thomas looks at me. Both of our eyes got wide and I thought I would pee in my pants, but I don't.

Cousin Sally got up from the chair and walks to the other room where Cousin Buddy was at.

I sigh a silent breath of relief knowing I didn't pee in my pants and knowing Cousin Sally is no longer in the room. I quickly began to think of food.

We're mostly hungry and tired. It was starting to get late and we hadn't eaten since breakfast this morning.

Just then Cousin Sally's voice interrupts my thoughts. "Stay in the house," she says. "We'll be back. We won't be gone but for a few minutes."

Thomas and I quickly said, "Okay."

Cousin Sally and Cousin Buddy walk out of the shack and down the ragged steps. She and Cousin Buddy got in the car and left.

THE DOG ANGEL

We stay inside the house like Cousin Sally told us to. It was dusk outside and it wasn't a lot of light inside either. Suddenly, a black dog appears from nowhere. It was a black dog with curly hair. It starts wagging its tail and floating all around.

Thomas and I look at each other. I blurt out, "Ooh, Thomas, look at the pretty dog. Where did it come from?"

Everywhere we went in the house the dog went too. We tried catching the dog but it seems like it was floating in the air. We could never touch or catch that dog, but we ran after that dog, and that dog ran after us.

I even look down at the floor, but I never see the dog's feet. We just ran and ran after that black dog, laughing and laughing.

I shout, "Thomas, get the dog! Get the dog Thomas!"

"I can't," laughs Thomas still running after the dog. "You get him," he said with outreached arms.

We have a good old time playing with that dog. We are happy!

After a while, Cousin Sally and Cousin Buddy came back. Cousin Sally has a brown paper sack that she began to open. When she lifts her hand from the bag she pulls out two coca cola bottles. We thought soda was in the bottles, but the bottles are empty.

Cousin Sally then takes out a container with kerosene in it and began pouring kerosene into each bottle. She took a long rag and twisted it and twisted it before stuffing it into the coca cola bottle. After making sure that the rag was drenched with kerosene and pulled up some in the bottle, she struck a wooden match and lit the rag. She made a homemade lantern out of coca cola bottles. Cousin Sally turns and looks at Thomas and me.

"Don't never touch this. This could be very dangerous," she said sternly to us.

She won't have to worry about me touching the kerosene lantern made from coca cola bottles. I was too scary.

Cousin Sally makes a pallet on the floor with a couple of old blankets. "Get down there, and go to sleep," she said pointing to the pallet on the floor.

And we did. We got down on the pallet and lay across it. We are glad to lie down. We don't have pajamas, so we slept in the clothing that we have on. We don't eat anything that night, but we are glad to finally lie down, especially after running around and chasing after the black dog.

Cousin Sally blew out the handmade lantern and set it on top of the empty mantel piece. There was nothing else on top of that old mantel piece but the coca cola lantern. Not even a frame with a picture in it. Cousin Sally blows out that lantern every night before going to bed.

Cousin Sally said good night and went towards the bedroom where Cousin Buddy was waiting. She walks carefully with the second coca cola lantern in one hand into the bedroom. She closes the door gently and quietly behind her.

Thomas and I held each other tightly. Not because it was cold, because it was still hot outside. We held each other because it was pitch, dark and scary. Suddenly, I thought of Momma.

When we got up the next morning, we saw Cousin Sally in the kitchen. She was putting wood in the wood burning stove. I could hear the wood crackling and see the white smoke escaping whenever she would open the stove door.

Thomas and I went into the kitchen. We don't have far to walk because the kitchen was right there. We're so hungry, and we are so ready to finally eat. We start watching Cousin Sally's every move.

We watch as she took some flour out of a bag and put it in a glass bowl. She then pours water into the bowl and stirs profusely. After that she pours a little batter in the hot greased pan on top of the stove. She waits a moment and then flips the flap jack or pancakes, as Thomas likes to call them, over on its other side. The smell of flap jacks soon began to eagerly fill the air.

Cousin Sally then motions for me to come closer and says, "This is how you make syrup."

She put some water in a pot and put it on the wood burning stove. Soon the water began to boil. She then takes a cup almost full of sugar and pours it into the water. Cousin Sally stirs and stirs and stirs.

I watch the water bubble and bubble until it got thick and thicker, then turn into syrup. Boy did it look yummy, I thought as I lick my lips.

Finally, Cousin Sally puts two little baby doll pancakes on each of our saucer. We don't have a plate, just a saucer. The pancakes are so small I guess a saucer is all that's needed.

She began to pour sugar syrup on our pancakes. I was hoping some of the syrup would slide off the pancakes on to my saucer but it doesn't. We ate with our hands because we aren't given a fork or spoon.

These flap jacks sure are good. I can eat five of them. I wish I had more sugar syrup. I want some more syrup, but I am too scared to ask for any. That's mostly all we ate every day, every day while at Cousin Sally's and Cousin Buddy's place.

Cousin Sally and Cousin Buddy always left the house around two or three o'clock in the afternoon. I guess they went to work each day, though they never tell us where they are going.

It's also kind of hard to tell what time it is without a clock or what day it is without a calendar. I am only eight, but Momma taught me how to judge time by looking at the sun in the sky. If the sun is in position above your head then it is high noon. It was after noon.

We are happy when they leave the shack because that's when the black dog appears. Every time Cousin Sally and Cousin Buddy left and the door closes behind them, the black dog came and would keep us company. The dog would disappear whenever they got back to the shack. Cousin Sally and Cousin Buddy never came back until late at night, like twelve, or one, or two in the morning. At least it seems like it was after midnight when they came home. Needless to say, we are chasing that black dog an awful lot. We are happy chasing that dog.

THE BEATING

After about a week, I guess, Thomas got a stomach ache. He was holding his stomach and was moaning and groaning and rocking back and forth. I felt sorry for him, because he hasn't had a bowel movement since we've been here. We've been eating two baby doll pancakes with sugar syrup daily, and he's probably constipated, I thought.

When Cousin Sally saw Thomas holding his stomach and rocking back and forth she gave him some castor oil to make his bowels move.

It made his bowels move alright, and Thomas doesn't make it to the outside in time. He boo booed on himself and began crying.

The shack began to fill up with boo boo smell. The smell lit up the room like a bright light. A wet puddle starts to form on the floor beneath Thomas' feet. Thomas looks so pitiful.

Cousin Sally looks our way suddenly. She could smell the stench in the air and knows what happened.

She turns toward Thomas and yells, "You done sh--t on yourself and I'm gonna' beat your a--."

She goes outside to get a switch. She picks a switch and soon came back into the shack. She starts walking toward Thomas holding the switch tightly in her right hand.

Thomas begins to tremble and cry. His whole body seems to tremble including his hair. His lips are trembling, his hands are trembling, and he was shaking like a leaf looking up at Cousin Sally as she stood over him.

I look at him and I feel so deeply hurt and tears start coming out of my eyes. I hold my head down low, so that Cousin Sally can't see me crying. I don't want her to beat me too. I slowly turn around away from them and cry silently.

Cousin Sally began to beat Thomas with the switch. I quickly turn around and see that it was one of those skinny green limbs. It looks like the kind that comes from a hedge bush that has not been trimmed in years. Thomas starts screaming and crying, trying to get away from the pain.

That's when Cousin Buddy screams at Cousin Sally from inside their bedroom.

"Leave them alone. That's what you brought them here for, to dog them?" he shouts in an angry voice.

"You have nothing to do with this. These are my d-mn people, not yours," Cousin Sally yells back at him and keeps beating Thomas.

Cousin Buddy shouts again and says, "Leave them d-mn kids alone. Stop that! What did you expect was going to happen after giving the boy castor oil?"

When we hear Cousin Buddy say that, we fell in love with him.

Cousin Sally stops beating Thomas and quickly marches into the bedroom where Cousin Buddy was at. They began fussing and fighting and knocking things around. We can hear a whole lot of banging and thumping going on. I was happy he was beating her up. Maybe now she would be too scared to beat on us.

Abruptly, the noise in the bedroom stops and they got to be lovey dovey again.

I can hear Cousin Buddy saying, "I didn't ever want to hurt you, but you can't be mean to the kids." Then we heard hugging and kissing, and moaning and groaning, and bumping.

Once Cousin Sally eventually came out of the bedroom, she gets a metal wash pan from underneath the tiny table in the center of the kitchen. She fills it with water from a bucket against the side of the wall and cleans Thomas up. She washes his clothes and hangs them on the wire fence that divides the shack from the cotton field and then told us that we can go outside and play.

Thomas goes outside first. I'm sure he is glad to get out of the shack and so was I. Cousin Sally has combed his hair, and he was looking very nice and clean.

He was in the middle of the yard, and I was at the corner of the house when I heard Cousin Sally saying in a soft whispering voice, "Don't move Thomas. Stand still."

I turn to look and see why Cousin Sally told Thomas not to move, when I see a big snake rattling its tail. It is gold and black. The snake was long and looks as if it was ready to pounce any minute. It was only inches away from Thomas.

Cousin Sally quietly, but quickly, got off the porch and went to the side of the house where the corn field is. She reaches out and grabs a couple of corn stalks that was close to her and yanks them both out of the ground at one time. She hurriedly went to where Thomas and the snake are, and she beat the snake like she had beaten Thomas. Only, she beat the snake to death with those corn stalks.

She then picks up the snake. But first she pokes it hard with a piece of one of the left over corn stalks that she had beaten it with, to make sure the snake was dead. After the snake didn't move, she bends down and picks it up. She places the snake on its back, on top of the wire fence with its stomach facing upward.

Wow, what a close call, I thought as I ran over to where Thomas stood. I grab him and hug him very tightly. I was so happy that the snake did not bite him. I thought about Momma. I always think about Momma when the going gets rough.

Soon we start to play but not for long. About an hour after Cousin Sally laid the snake belly up on the wire fence it began thundering. Thomas and I ran inside.

Once inside it starts raining and thundering and lightening so fiercely, it seems like the shack began to tremble. Kind of like when Thomas was trembling before his beating, uncontrollably.

It starts raining really hard. It looks like an ocean falling from the sky. It rains hard for three or four straight hours. It was as if the sky became angry and the heavens open up and drenched the earth with tears.

After the rain finally stops, Cousin Sally and Uncle Buddy left. As soon as they left the black dog appears. Thomas and I began to chase and run after the dog. Then the dog began to chase and run after us. We laugh and laugh because we can never catch that dog. Come to think of it, that dog could never catch us either. We are very happy chasing the dog even though we are beginning to get homesick.

THE DEVIL AND THE WATER

Thomas and I soon learn that we are responsible for fetching water. Fetching water was no easy task. We had to walk down the deep, steep steps that led from the front porch to the dirt road below.

Thomas and I can barely walk down or climb the steps. They are so steep. I feel so very sorry for Thomas. He is just a little boy and small for his age. Fetching water became a routine, one which we barely could manage.

We don't drink a lot of water, because we never have a lot at one time. Thomas and I can't carry much water either. It's too heavy for us to carry without wasting it, but we try not to bring the containers back empty. We drink as much water as we can when we go fetch it.

Cousin Sally gave us a gallon jug and a gallon jar to put the water in. I carry the jar and Thomas carries the jug. I gave Thomas the jug because it has a handle on it and he can drag it, since he can't carry it.

We get our water from around the back of the big white house we stopped at when we first got here. The house where I saw the old man and the old lady standing in the back yard watching us leave that day.

Though I never saw them outside again, since that first day, I sometimes would hear them inside the house talking or moving around, like today. I can't make out what they're saying, but they don't say anything to us.

We walk around the back of the house and get water from the faucet. I don't fill our gallon jug and jar completely to the top with water, because we won't be able to carry it; so I fill them almost half full.

Thomas drags his gallon jug by the handle behind him. I carry my gallon jar carefully with both of my hands, unless I have to hold Thomas' hand. We're scared of breaking the jug or jar, and we don't want to bring them back empty.

I remember our first day fetching water. Cousin Sally said, "You better not break this jug or jar. If you break them I'm going to beat the hell out of you."

Cousin Sally then walks us halfway to the big white house that first day we got water. She stops at a square piece of concrete with an opening in the middle of the ground and points at it.

"You see this", she said peering down at us.

I shift my eyes from hers and look at the concrete. And Thomas looks too.

Still pointing at the concrete Cousin Sally said, "This is called a dip in that."

I want to look at Thomas, but we don't look at one another. We just stare down at the concrete with the opening in the center. I was too scared to look at Cousin Sally.

Then she says in an evil voice, "If you try to run away, it's the devil down there, and he's gonna get you and drag you down to hell. If you try to run away, he gonna' burn your a-- up."

She points her finger at the dip in the concrete. She scared me so badly that day that my heart starts feeling funny.

I thought about that day as Thomas and I kept getting closer and closer to the piece of concrete where the devil lives. Cousin Sally called it a dip in that. At least that's what it sounded like she called it to me. I was always too scared to ask her to repeat herself.

Thomas and I slow down, like we do every time we see the dip in that. Thomas looks at me and I look at him. Suddenly, something says, "grrrrrrrh, grrrrrrrh."

We got so scared and start running away from the devil. We still held on to the jar and jug though. We almost had a bowel movement on ourselves. We finally look back but don't see the devil behind us. After today, we always cross the road when we fetch water, so we won't be on the same side where the devil lives.

We learn later on which animal had made that noise. It was a frog that made the noise and not the dreaded devil.

THE TWO ESCAPES

Time seem to fly and yet stand still. We must have been here for at least a month now. We are always hungry. More hungry than if we were at home with Momma. Even though we are poor, Momma would always try to feed us. We are beginning to get tired of always being alone at night. We want to go home.

We're just tired of being here, especially because of Cousin Sally's ways. After Thomas' beating, we got really scared of being around her.

She put so much fear in me that I can't look at her. I keep my head down. She always keeps trying to look me in the eyes. When she does that, I start blinking my eyes really fast because I am so scared of her. I am so nervous when she is around, and I'm never sure what she might suddenly do.

"Stop blinking your d-mn eyes like a cat," Cousin Sally snaps at me.

I still can't look at her. I almost pee on myself, because I am so scared; but I went outside and peed instead.

I was ready to leave the shack. I was scared to go but scared to stay.

One afternoon around three o'clock, Cousin Sally and Cousin Buddy left us alone again. I scrummage up enough nerves to try and escape.

"Come on Thomas, let's leave." I said looking at Thomas.

Thomas says, "Okay."

We then began to slowly squeeze through the opening between the big trunk that was used for the front door. Down the steps we went. My heart was thumping so fast and hard that I thought I would pass out.

Once we reach the bottom, we don't go toward the dirt road. I grab Thomas' hand and we ran through the back yard toward the woods. I figure no one will see us in the back.

We walk toward a clearing in the woods. We are walking really fast when we saw a lake. We are almost upon the lake when we hear a noise and a big, big splash.

It sounds like an alligator to me, I thought. I got really scared and turn toward Thomas.

"Thomas let's go back. I'm scared the alligator will get us and kill us," I said feeling very afraid.

I grab his hand tighter and we speed walked back to the shack. We again squeeze back through the small opening by the big trunk that was used as the front door of the shack.

When we got inside the black dog appears. We laugh and we play with the dog. We are always happy chasing that dog. That dog makes us very, very happy.

We are wide awake when Cousin Sally and Uncle Buddy came in. We usually stay awake until they got home, because we are too scared to fall asleep.

Cousin Sally would make us go to bed whenever she came in.

We got on our pallet and I close my eyes. Well, we didn't escape from the shack, I thought as I lay there quite exhausted in the dark. But at least we escaped the alligator.

THE ANGEL IN THE CAR

About a week later, I decide it's time to pray. Thomas and I would always see Momma pray. Momma prays an awful lot too. She would pray for hours and hours. Sometimes, we would get on our knees and pray with Momma. Momma always said that if you need help pray, and ask God to help you. She said, "God will help you." I sure miss Momma.

I remember Momma said that I was born with a veil on my face. Yes, a veil covering my face. The old folks say that if you are born with a veil, you can see and hear things that other people can't.

I was born at Devoy Medical Center in Jacksonville, Florida. I was born with veil, a covering over my face. I've been told that the doctor pulled the veil away from around my nose and mouth, so I could breathe. The doctor left the veil covering my eyes and it dried up and came off on its own after a while.

… Most people today probably have never heard of being born with a veil. I guess it's a thing of the past or the doctors just don't let you know anymore.

…

When I look up from my thoughts, Thomas is standing in front of me.

I say in an excited voice, "Come on Thomas. Hold my hands and let's pray!"

Thomas says, "Okay!" and grabs my hands. We hold hands tightly.

I said, "Jesus! Please, please let somebody come and get us Jesus! Amen!"

"Amen," Thomas echoes. We feel happy!

About one week later, we decide to go outside on the front porch to play. We're not supposed to be outside on the porch, but that day we went outside anyway. We start running around in a circle, not fast, but we are beginning to get a little dizzy.

Suddenly, we stop playing and began walking toward the steps. We start going down the steps. We made it down three steps before we decide to turn around. We got scared and didn't want to get caught outside, so we go back into the house and began playing with the dog.

Several days later we go back on the porch after Cousin Sally and Cousin Buddy left. That's when the Angel in the car came driving by as fast as lightning on the dirt road below. That car had to be going about eighty or ninety miles an hour.

"Whoosh!" was all we heard.

The car was going so fast and kicking up so much dust that that's all we saw below was dust. We can see dust for several miles down the road from where we stood on the hill. At least it looks like several miles down the road.

Then the car unexpectedly stops. It came to a screeching halt and starts backing up. It was backing up just as fast as it did when it passed by, kicking up a cloud of dust.

The car swiftly stops in front of the steps below. I could see a woman leaning from the driver's side, reach over and quickly roll down the window on the passenger side.

It was a brown skin lady with a wide smile. She puts her head out of the window and looks up at us.

She says, "Hi."

I say, "Hi."

She says, "Are you Ms. Annabelle's granddaughter?"

I say, "Yes," then start crying like a baby.

Through my tears I ask the lady, "Will you please tell my grandmother to come and get me?"

The brown skin lady smiles and says, "I sure will baby," and she was gone just like the wind, kicking up more dust.

When she left, we can't see nothing but the top of the car through all that dust. We start playing again but then decide to go back inside. We don't want Cousin Sally to catch us outside.

Thomas and I squeeze between the trunk that's in the doorway and went back inside the shack. Once we got inside the shack the dog appears. The dog would always come from behind us and then run in front of us. The dog never follows us outside though.

We start running after the dog, trying to catch it. We are just laughing and laughing, having a good old time. We are happy.

THE RESCUE

About two days later we woke up early. It was a usual day and starts out like any other day. We ate our two little pancakes with sugar syrup around noon like we do just about every day. Cousin Sally and Cousin Buddy left together around the same time as always.

The black dog appears from behind, just like it did the nights before. Thomas and I are chasing the dog when there is a knock on the trunk.

"Bang! Bang! Bang!"

"Who is it?" I ask even though I am scared to death. We never get visitors, but I felt I had to say something.

"Annabelle. Open up." A female voice answers.

It is my Grandma Annabelle. Grandma Annabelle to the rescue I thought. I was so happy to hear her voice that I start crying.

Thomas and I try moving the trunk, but we can't. The trunk is bigger than both of us put together. We would always squeeze around the side of the trunk to go in and out of the house.

That's when Uncle Charlie, who had driven grandma to get us, reaches his arm through the opening and throws aside the trunk. Just like that. The trunk lands on the side of the wall with a loud thump.

Grandma Annabelle walks in and says, "Get your stuff. Let's go."

I reply, "Okay."

Then I asked, "Big Momma," that's what I sometimes call her, "Was that lady your friend who I told to tell you to come get me?"

"I've never seen that lady before in my life." Grandma said.

I look at her in wide eyed disbelief. Surely, she had to know the brown skin lady with the pretty wide smile. After all, the lady mentioned Grandma Annabelle by name.

"Was she your friend?" I ask Grandma again.

Grandma repeats, "No, I told you that I never seen that lady before."

I asked, "Did she come and tell you what I said?"

"Yes, ma'am." Grandma replies motioning us to come on.

Since Grandma Annabelle doesn't know the lady, I figure the lady must have been an Angel. She was the Angel in the car.

I was smiling as I hurriedly grab my dress and about three other pieces of our clothing. That's all we have with us.

We left. We left the rotten old shack. We left the trunk pushed over to the side away from the door. We left the lantern burning on top of the empty mantel piece. We left the stuffed, unmade pallet that we slept on. We left the water bucket, empty in the middle of the kitchen floor. We left the baby doll pancakes and sugar syrup that we ate every day. We left the black dog too. We did want to take the black dog with us, but the dog didn't appear. So, we just left. This is the happiest day of my life.

Big Momma took us to her house in Georgia. Grandma Annabelle is my Momma's mother, and Momma and Uncle Charlie are brother and sister.

Once we got to Big Momma's house, Grandma phones a cousin in Jacksonville, Florida. I heard her say, "Tell Daisy," my Momma, "that I found them. I have Thomas and Frances," Big Momma said triumphantly.

I guess Cousin Sally and Cousin Buddy never knew what happened to us. We never saw them again. Not to see Cousin Sally again was indeed the happiest day of my young life.

Then about five years later, Momma hears that Cousin Sally has died.

I wonder what ever happened to Cousin Buddy. We liked Cousin Buddy a lot, especially after he defended us. I hope that he is okay.

MOMMA DAISY

Almost a month later, Momma comes to Georgia where we are at. We all are living with Big Momma. Momma works very, very hard each day and saves her money. She works for white folks, cooking, scrubbing, and cleaning. She was good at what she did, and the people like her work.

She saves enough money to buy the lot across the street from Big Momma. Momma finally owns her own property, and she was mighty proud.

She has a man named Mr. Kimble build us a house. Although Mr. Kimble uses a cane to walk with, he builds us a house with one huge room in it. He doesn't get a chance to add walls, because Mr. Kimble soon got sick and was never able to finish the house. He eventually dies. Needless to say, our house never got finish, but it was a nicely built house.

We can make three rooms out of that one big room, but Momma only makes two rooms. We hung up bed sheets to divide the bedroom from the kitchen. We use the sheets like doors. It gave us a little more privacy, but how much privacy can you have in one room.

Someone gave Momma two regular size beds, so she don't have to buy beds right now. Momma had a bed to herself, and we children share the other bed. It was nice to sleep in a soft bed, even if I share it with my other siblings. That's better than sleeping on the floor most times.

Though at times, I would make a pallet on the floor for myself. I was the oldest and I need a little privacy at times. I would pile blankets and sometimes even clothing on the floor and sleep on top of it. Sometimes, pallets are so comfortable to me, and plus, I like sleeping by myself.

Momma continues working hard washing and ironing laundry, cleaning houses and cooking meals for white folks. She would sometimes work day and night. She was proud of her work and she likes saving her money.

One of the first things Momma does buy is an armoire. She always wanted one. An armoire is used to hang clothing in. Like a fancy closet in the middle of the room. Momma's armoire has a long drawer at the bottom to put your underwear in. Momma don't have a lot of underwear to put in the drawer. None of us have a lot of underwear, though Momma probably has more than me.

Her armoire is beautiful. It is made of fine wood and has a mirror in the front. It's made from the good wood. Oak, I think. It has knobs on it that shines like gold and a key to lock it with. Momma adores her armoire.

The next thing Momma bought was a table and four chairs. We have never had a table and four chairs before. Now, when Momma cooks meals, we sometimes will sit at the table in the kitchen and watch. When it was time for meals, we all sat down at the table and ate. That is after we say grace, of course. We feel blessed.

The third thing Momma saves her money for is a double barrel shot gun. She bought one. She keeps that gun at the head of her bed, on the side that she sleeps on. Momma told us kids never to touch that gun. We never do. So far, she hasn't had to use that double barrel shot gun but she was ready.

We like living in our house. We never had a house of our own, and we thought we were rich. I especially enjoy living across the street from Big Momma.

Big Momma and I are very close. I don't have anyone to play with, so I would often go over Big Momma's and climb the big, big tree in her back yard. I would wrap my legs around a limb and hang backwards with my head hanging toward the ground. That's how I spent a lot of my spare time, hanging at Big Momma's.

Momma soon began to have problems with her eyes. The doctor says she has glaucoma and that she would never see again.

Momma prays and prays. She prays day and night and night and day. She prays so hard and her sight came back after about one month. She could see again.

I'm beginning to see how prayer works. Momma prayed for her eyesight to return, and it did return. Thomas and I prayed that Jesus would send somebody to get us from the shack. We prayed just like Momma taught us, and Big Momma came and rescued us from the shack. Momma always says to ask God, and God will help you. Almighty God did help us.

I guess that shows how powerful prayer can be. The power of prayer is amazing. We are happy. We have an awful lot to be thankful for.

THE DOG PAN

That brings me back to another memory I have of how prayer works and can bring about change.

I'm remembering how Momma was praying all the time. A lot of nights, I woke up and Momma is on the side of the bed praying. She don't talk to a lot of people; because she is always in the house praying, if she's not working for others.

Momma has glaucoma in her eyes and it was getting worse again. That's what eventually takes her sight. The foods we eat don't help her glaucoma none.

We ate a lot of starchy foods like white rice, white bread, white sugar; whatever we can get our hands on. The doctor said those food are not good for Momma to eat. That's all we have to eat most times, because it was cheap.

We don't really have a lot to eat sometimes, especially when Momma's eye sight would come and go. The doctors told Momma that she will never see again.

Before Momma went blind, she took us kids with her and walks to try and find work. Momma walks up to this one house; while us kids wait in the background, and knocks on the front door. When the door opens, a white couple is standing there and just stares at Momma.

Momma told the white couple, "My children are hungry. If you have any old cold food from yesterday that you don't want, I will work for it so my kids can eat."

They look at each other and finally the white lady said, "Hold on."

Then she goes into the house and closes the door behind her.

The white man said, "I may have a little work for you to do," and he walks toward this big huge tree facing acres of cotton.

Momma and I follow the man towards the big tree. The man points pass the tree to the cotton field and then gave us a couple of hoes to chop weeds with.

While following the white man, I look to the right and notice that there is a dog chained by the back door. I'm glad the dog is friendly, I was thinking. I then look down and saw the dog's pan that the dog ate out of. It was gray with black spots and looks dirty with old yucky, hard stuff on it.

After Momma put my little brother and sister under the big huge tree, we immediately began working.

I would sometimes make excuses to break, so that I can check on the younger ones under the tree. Most times, I would say that I need to get some water. I would grab the big jar; that we always took to the fields with us; and I would head to the water faucet. We use the big jar to put water in.

We were working so hard that we never seen the white lady come out of the house. She had put some food in a pan and had given it to my little brother and my little sister, Baby Teen, as they sat under the big tree. I noticed them eating something.

I continue to the water faucet which is in the back by the dog. I notice that the dog's pan had disappeared. I fill the jar with water and start walking back to the field.

I look at the kids to make sure they are still okay, when I notice what they are eating out of. It looks just like they are eating out of the dog's pan. I remember looking at that dog's pan earlier. The pan was grey with black spots on it, just like what the kids are eating out of now.

We had gone to the fields to work only to come back to find the younger kids eating out of the dog's pan. They are almost finished eating whatever is in the pan.

I went quickly back to where Momma was working and said, "Momma she gave them food in the dog's pan." I wrinkle my nose in disgust.

Momma said, "Well, they ate it already. It won't hurt them. Nothing can be done."

Another time I said that I needed some water, so that I could go check on the kids. When I got to the water faucet, I notice that the pan the kids were eating out of was put back by the dog. That's when I knew for sure they had eaten out of the dog's pan. I just continue filling the jar with water and went back to the field.

We continue chopping weeds from the cotton field, for hours, with a hoe. A hoe has a long wooden thin handle, with a sharp flat metal piece, at the end of it. It can be used to chop weeds from in between and around plants. It can also be used to dig a hole in the dirt to plant seeds or plants. It can even be used to kill a snake with also, if you have too.

I look down at my hands. They had already started to blister some from holding the hoe so tightly and from working so hard. I'm sure Momma's hands were looking and feeling the same way. We work all day long. We chop that whole cotton field.

When we finally finish chopping, the white man came to us. He gave Momma three dollars and he gave me three dollars. Momma thanks him and gathers up my little brother and Baby Teen and we left.

We went straight to the market before it closes. I bought clothes with my three dollars. I even bought a pretty dress for fifty cents.

… That's right, just fifty cents! You can't buy a dress for fifty cents nowadays!

By the way, the kids did get sick. They had gotten a stomach virus soon after they had eaten out of the dog's pan that the white lady had given to them. Momma gave the kids herbs to help get rid of whatever they had, and she prayed a lot. …

Momma bought food with her three dollars. You can buy a lot of food with three dollars. She bought white flour, white rice, grits, and corn meal.

Momma also bought a lot of chicken. That is a lot of chicken necks, chicken backs, chicken gizzards, chicken livers, and chicken feet. We can't afford to buy the whole chicken only the chicken parts.

Momma would take and boil the chicken necks until they were nice and tender and most times falling off the bone. Sometimes, it was our main course, but not often. Most of the time, we put the chicken necks in our beans or cabbage or rice. We ate chicken necks that way a lot.

Momma would fry the chicken gizzards and livers in a little oil, if we had oil; and we would eat them like that. If Momma cooks the gizzards and livers this way, it was what we call a treat. I like the gizzards much better than the livers. The chicken livers are so soft and mushy and taste funny in my mouth.

Momma would cook the chicken feet too. They are used to season the rice and soup with mostly. They are good also, especially when you're hungry. Chicken feet don't have a lot of meat on them though.

We ate for a few weeks off that food. We are happy. Then Momma went blind.

THE BALL IN THE DITCH

Both of Momma's eyes went dark. It happen about three weeks after we worked for cold and old, yesterday's food. It happen just like the doctor's said it would. It seems Momma will never see again.

… Momma went blind a few times, but she never went to a doctor again for many, many years after she went all the way blind. She would use herbs and prayers for medicine and she lived to be 95 years old.

Her Momma, Grandma Annabelle or Big Momma as I sometimes called her, lived to be 111 years old. The newspaper has Big Momma's age at 107; but the family says she was older than that. I guess the family ought to know. Big Momma didn't have a birth certificate.

I took care of Momma until she passed on. I sure do miss Momma and my Big Momma. …

Anyway, after Momma went all the way blind again, we don't have anyone to really look after us. Momma does the best she can, but it was hard to do for us kids, especially when she can't see. Daddy was always in and out of the house so much that Momma finally told him to leave.

It is a very hot day today, and I sure wish I had something cold to drink. I was thinking how fortunate we are that we have an icebox.

… We didn't have a refrigerator back then. We had what was called an ice box. That's where you put a large block of ice on a tray or compartment inside a wooden box like structure. The wooden structure was typically lined with tin. We would put a foot tub underneath the ice to catch the water when the ice melted. The ice had to be replaced whenever it melted, so that the food could stay cold and the tub emptied, so that it wouldn't overflow. Time sure does bring about a change. …

The day is a smoking hot, and I sure wish I had five cents. For five cents I can buy a big block of ice. Sometimes, we wouldn't buy ice because five cents would also buy a lot of pork neck bones too. But it got to a point where we can't buy ice or food after Momma went blind.

Momma began to pray really hard. All day and all night long she would pray. I would hear her pray throughout the night, and I would start to cry.

One night I fell down on my knees beside her and prayed hard like Momma. I start repeating everything Momma would say. Big tears were streaming from my eyes. We prayed and prayed all night, and afterwards we both went to bed.

Momma wakes me up around five o'clock in the morning before the sun came out.

"Frances!" Momma said most anxiously and excitedly. "Go and get the money that God has shown me!"

Momma would have gone herself, but she can't see anymore.

"I'm scared," I said with fear in my voice.

It's still dark outside and there are no street lights on our street. I was scared to go outside by myself so early in the morning.

Momma said, "Don't be scared. God's gonna' be right with you."

She then gives me precise instructions and tells me what to do.

She said in a matter of fact voice, "Walk straight up the road and make sure that you stay on the left hand side of the street.

"When you see Ms. Blackmore's house, stop and look down in the ditch, and get the money. It's a big ball of money, about the size of a grapefruit. It has lots of rubber bands around it."

I said, "Okay", and open the front door.

I began slowly walking down the street. I look up at the sky and saw the moon shining, but it was the stars that were truly shining so very brightly. The stars were shining so brightly that I did not have any trouble seeing in front of me at all. I pick up my pace with confidence and start walking faster.

I went down the street like Momma told me, making sure that I stay on the left side of the road. I briefly stand in front of Ms. Blackmore's house. I don't want to stand there too long for fear someone will see me.

I then look down in the ditch. It isn't really a ditch. The ditch is where the road scraper dug too deeply in the road. I think I see something. I look closer and there it was. A big ball of money in the ditch, just like Momma said.

I reach into the ditch and grab the money. It was a big ball of money with rubber bands wrapped all around it. It was the biggest ball of money that I ever saw.

I held the money against my chest. I held it with one hand, and I swiftly put my other hand over that hand to make sure the money did not fall out. I start running down the street towards home.

I yell running triumphantly down the middle of the street, "I got it Momma! I got it!"

… If anyone saw or heard me back then, they probably thought I was crazy, but they would not have believed what happened anyway. …

I wonder how Momma knew about the money. Sometimes, Momma would have dreams that came true. It was as if she has special powers. She always praised God for everything.

I was feeling mighty proud of myself. I gave that big ball of money to Momma. Momma is able to feed us now. We are able to eat for a long, long time on that money.

THE GOLD COINS

The big ball of money lasted for months and months, but eventually we were hungry again. Momma was always praying. One day, when she was on her knees, she prays these words.

"Jesus. Please give me money to feed my little children." She prays so hard, as she rocks back and forth.

Then she tells me, "God showed me where money is. It's a million dollars and it's in a white neighborhood. An old white lady used to live there and she died. I used to work for her.

"God showed me where the money is. The white lady's Spirit came to me and said I want you to have this and told me where a metal box was buried in her back yard by a tree. It's filled with gold coins the white lady's Spirit said."

After Momma finishes talking, she says "Come baby with me to get the money."

"Momma, please don't go up there to that white lady's house," I beg as tears start to form in my eyes.

I was scared. Even though the white lady is dead, I still had a grave concerns about this, and I don't want Momma to go. I feel that something bad will happen.

Momma was determined to go, and I went with her. She feels the gold coins are meant for us to have, if there were any coins at all. It starts raining on the way. When it starts to rain, I start to cry again.

"Momma, please don't go. Them folks gonna kill us." I blurt out through my tears as I continue to stumble through the rain. The rain was falling down fast like the tears on my face.

I kept on crying and telling Momma that something bad is going to happen to us. We have walked almost halfway there. We are just about to go to where the new highway starts when Momma finally listens to me. We turn around and we walk back to the house. I was so thankful and relieved that we are not going to that white lady's house!

About two weeks later the white lady house was being torn down. It was said that the people who tore it down heard that gold was on the land. They went back to the white lady's house and start digging for the gold.

According to the radio and newspaper, they found the gold. It was a million dollars in gold coins! Just like Momma had said! A million dollars in gold coins could have been all ours. If only I hadn't talked Momma into turning around.

Momma continues to feel that the gold coins were meant for us. All those gold coins would have been nice to have. Momma blamed me for years for not getting the gold, but we survived.

THE BARON

After we didn't get the gold, The Baron came into Momma's life. He is nice to Momma and thinks she is pretty. He likes us kids, and we like The Baron a lot. When he came into our lives, we went from the darkness to the light, when it came to food.

He told Momma that he is from South Carolina. He brings us food, and he gives Momma pretty gifts. The Baron pays a lot of attention to Momma, and he gives us kids attention too. We are very fortunate that The Baron came into our lives.

The Baron eventually got a job working for these rich white people. One day, the rich white people prepare to give a grand Christmas party for about three hundred people. Three hundred of their friends, family, neighbors, and business partners all have invitations to come.

The decorations and tables are immaculate. The tables held fancy china and silverware and all kinds of fancy food on it. Raw food, cooked food, whole hams, whole yams, whole chickens, whole green beans, whole corn on the cob, and many types of fruits and nuts are on that table. That's how The Baron describes it.

The Baron said that the white people left the house and he helps himself. He helps himself to the silverware, the plates, the whole chickens, the whole hams, the whole green beans, the whole corn on the cob, the fruits and nuts, the decorations, and even the table cloths.

The Baron clears the table and gives the food to people who don't have food. He took the many beautiful gifts also and gave them away. He was the black Santa Claus to people in the neighborhood that year.

He gave Momma china and many different beautiful gifts. The Baron gave me a white doll. That was my Christmas present. It was the first doll I ever had and the last. I kept that doll and loved it. I kept it for a long time. That doll was more precious to me than Momma's expensive gifts. He gave the other kids gifts also.

We ate for many months off the food he gave us that day. We have whole chickens and lots of whole hams. Imagine having a whole chicken instead of just the chicken necks or feet. It has everything on it except the chicken's feet. What a treat that is.

There are all kinds of fruit and all kinds of candy that The Baron gave us. He gave us kids the biggest candy cane I had ever saw before. This is the best Christmas ever in my whole life. We all are so very happy.

Then one day, soon after Christmas was over, I was standing in the yard, and I saw The Baron in the back of a police car. As the car passed by, The Baron raised his handcuffed hands, waves and mouths the words bye bye, bye bye to me. I read his lips.

I ran into the house as fast as I could and tells Momma what happened and what I had seen. We felt very sad for The Baron. We know we probably will never see him again and we don't.

Momma continues to pray and pray each and every day. Eventually, her eye sight began to come back. Eventually, she began to see again.

… Momma went blind a few times in her life. Her eye sight came back every time except for the last time. Each time her eye sight came back, she was grateful. …

Then three weeks later, Momma bought a newspaper because she saw The Baron's picture on the front page of the newspaper. She had someone else read the article to her, because Momma can't read.

The newspaper mentions that The Baron was an escaped prisoner who has been recaptured. It also mentions that The Baron was made to go to each house that he had taken the white folk's presents to get the presents back.

That is everybody's house except ours. He didn't tell them about us and the police never came to our house. They only passed by.

We are really sad for The Baron. I cried because he was so nice to Momma and us. I'll always remember the white doll he gave me.

It was another three months later when we hear on the radio that The Baron had been beaten to death. The radio and TV made it seem as if another inmate had beaten The Baron to death.

Folks here often wonder if it was the police who beat him to death for stealing those rich white folks stuff and giving it to black folks. Nobody will ever forget this Christmas. I know I won't.

THE TRAINED CHICKENS

About a year later, Momma buys another lot. It is located two or three blocks away from our house, at least I think it is. I just know that it isn't very far from Big Momma's house. Momma has our house moved from one lot to another. So, we kept the same unfinished house. I love my unfinished home. We are so grateful.

Momma starts raising chickens. She has about fifteen chickens now. Some of the chickens hatch from eggs that another chicken laid. I remember when my favorite chicken hatches. It is black and grey.

I was holding the chick in the palm of my hand when Momma said, "You can have that one. That one is yours," she said again.

I smile and call it Chicky Chick. I fell in love with that chicken and treat it like a pet. All of the chickens are treated like pets. We can call the chickens and play with them. They don't run. They come right up to us and get into our arms. Imagine that.

Those chickens went everywhere. They went to the neighbor's house. They went to the next neighbor's house up the street and down the street. They went everywhere. The neighbors don't seem to mind the chickens being everywhere. I mean everywhere.

Momma feeds the chickens twice a day. We kids peel the hard corn from the cob and Mom would feed the chickens with it. When it was time to feed the chickens, Momma would step outside the door and whistle loudly.

Those chickens would come running and I mean fast. It didn't matter if they were a block away; those chickens came flying down the street when Momma whistles.

Momma has the chickens trained that way. She trains them as soon as they hatch. It's so amazing to me how these chickens respond to Momma. All the people in the neighborhood are amazed by how good Momma has her chickens trained.

Sometimes, Momma would be walking down the street and the chickens would walk behind her in a straight line. One chicken after the other chicken, they'd walk following Momma down the street.

One day, when money and food was low, I came home and my favorite chicken was chicken and dumplings.

I should have known something was wrong because Chicky Chick did not greet me when I came home. I was use to Chicky Chick coming to me as soon as I got home. This day my pet chicken did not come greet me.

"Where is Chicky Chick?" I ask Momma.

"In there on the table," Momma replied in her matter of fact voice.

"On the table," I said.

Momma said, "Baby, we didn't have anything to eat. I had to kill it, so we can have something to eat."

I ran out of the kitchen. Needless to say, I didn't eat dinner that night. I couldn't see myself eating Chicky Chick. I cried for days over that chicken. I really liked Chicky Chick, but not in dumplings.

THE WHITE ANGEL GIRL

Momma continues to struggle even though she works hard. My Momma's sister and her family came to visit us from New Jersey. When it was time for them to leave, Momma asks them to take me back to New Jersey with them.

I don't really want to go; but Momma feels it was best, especially, since she is having a hard time feeding us. I guess she figures I was one less mouth she had to struggle to feed.

So, off to New Jersey I went. I try to fit in, but I was always by myself. No one wants to play with me. If it wasn't for my younger cousins, I wouldn't have anyone to play with.

One day, I was babysitting my younger cousins. After they fell asleep, I decide to go outside to play. I was minding my own business when Sonny, a boy in the neighborhood, came by and just stood staring at me.

He didn't do anything to me at all. He just stood there staring.

"What are you staring at with your ugly, snotty nose, black self," I blurts out.

Sonny continues to stand there and stare at me. His nose was snotty and he looks scared.

Suddenly, I push Sonny because he wouldn't stop looking at me. I push him on the side of his head.

He staggers sideways. Then he turns around and runs away crying. As he was running away, he ran right pass a white girl who was coming towards me at a fast pace. She has long blonde hair, and she has on a light color skirt and blouse that matches.

The white Angel Girl hit me upside my head in the same area that I had pushed Sonny. I try my best to hit her back, but my arms can never reach her. Her arms were longer than mine, and she hit me every time she hit at me.

I call her a Spirit because I can never touch the white Angel Girl no matter how hard I try. The Angel Girl came from nowhere. It seem like her feet never touches the ground, as she punches my head in.

That Spirit beat the mess out of me. She beat me all upside my head. After she gets through beating me really good, the white Angel Girl turns and walks away. She disappears just as fast as she appeared.

I don't tell anyone what happened because I am scared that I would get a whooping for pushing Sonny for no reason. I kept it to myself, but I will never forget it and neither will my head.

After that, I try to be friends with Sonny. He doesn't want anything to do with me, and I don't blame him. Never the less, I never bothered anyone again who didn't bother me.

… I see Sonny again when I am grown. He is a cab driver and he picked me up one day.

I said, "Hi Sonny."

He said, "Hi."

I said, "Do you remember me from Essex Street?"

Sonny replies, "Yes."

I said, "That white girl who beat me up when I pushed you must have been your girlfriend."

Sonny said, "No, what white girl?" He has a perplexed look on his face.

"A white girl beat me up for messing with you that day. As soon as you turned around that day, she appeared and beat the hell out of me with her fist, like a boxer," I said trying to get him to remember.

"I didn't have a white girlfriend. I don't know what you are talking about," Sonny replies while carefully driving the cab.

"Are you sure?" I ask. "You all passed right by each other," I said.

By now, I was pretty sure that he had not seen the white Angel Girl. After that, Sonny and I became friends and would talk whenever we saw each other. I am always glad to see him. He is a nice, friendly guy, and he always has a smile on his face. …

THE BUS THAT CRASHED

I grow up and eventually move back to Florida in my early twenties. This time I live in Fort Pierce, Florida. I have a good reason for moving here. My Dad lives here. This is the first time that I have ever seen my real Daddy.

His name is Nathaniel. I call him Nathaniel when we are just talking. When I want something from him, like money, I call him Daddy. That melts his heart and he would give me whatever I ask for, which wasn't a lot. I was happy to meet my Daddy.

Daddy Nathaniel rented me an apartment. My apartment has one big room like a kitchenette, except the bathroom and shower is outside in another building. I share the bathroom with about six other residents.

The building where the showers are located is like an army camp. It has a lot of showers, lined up in rows, in one open room. I would quickly take my shower and leave. I often times would fill a bucket with water and tote it to my apartment. I would wash up in my apartment on the days that I have water.

The toilets are located in another room. It is an open room also. Oh well, at least I have my own apartment. I like having my own everything.

Daddy Nathaniel lives not far from me. His apartment building is about ten feet from my apartment building. His apartment has a bathroom with a shower in it. Actually, each apartment in his whole apartment building has bathrooms and showers in it. I like to sometimes hang out in Daddy's apartment because of the bathroom conveniences.

But, I also like my own. I like my own apartment, with or without a bathroom. I love to work to have my own money. It makes me feel good not to ask anybody for anything. The only body I like asking for something from is The Almighty.

I got a job by showing up at what is called the loading zone. It is a big empty lot where lots of people would come to look for work. The lot is empty for a moment and then all the out of work folks would start to fill the lot. People would show up as early as four in the morning. You are lucky if you are selected.

Most of the work is farm work. There are different jobs to go to, and it always helps if that job was looking for a lot of people. That increases your chances of being selected.

I was one of the lucky ones. I got chosen to work on a tomato farm. This job pays more than most of the other jobs; and I am glad I landed it.

Everyone who is picked to work got on a bus that would take us from the loading dock to our jobs each day. Sometimes, I would fall asleep and so would others. The bus driver woke us up when we got to our destination. We arrive at the job site, the farm, by six in the morning and left at two in the afternoon.

… Today, I guess, this type of gathering for work would be called an employment agency. Sort of like Minutemen Temporary Agency and others. Even today a company may offer transportation to the job site. Usually, that transportation is on a bus or maybe an SUV, now days.

Sometimes, people do get hired on permanently. Still, even today, a lot of employment is temporary or you have a six months' probation period. Isn't it something how time change, but not really change at all. …

One of my job duties is to cut tomato suckers. Tomato suckers are small shoots that grow out from under where the stem and the branch of a tomato plant meet. I cut the tomato suckers off with a sharp razor so that the tomato would have room to grow.

Part of my job, also, is to put a stake in the ground by the tomatoes. This is done by sticking a stick in the ground next to each tomato plant. I would then attach the tomato stalk to the stick or stake, as it is sometimes called. After that, the stalk is secured to the stick with what looks like bread wire from a loaf of bread. This is hard work, but I like my job. Most of all, I like making my own money.

Meanwhile, I soon realize that I am allergic to tomatoes. I broke out almost everywhere with small little bumps. Bumps are on my face, my arms, and my legs. Little fine bumps are all over me.

I want to quit. This job pays the most money, so I stuck with it. I would put different salves on my skin hoping the salves would help get rid of the bumps and soothe my skin. It helped some but not much.

When I got the job, working with tomatoes, I was so happy. I enjoy getting out of the house. I truly enjoy making my own money. God is good!

One morning, I got up around three to get dressed to go to the loading dock for work. I usually wake up around this time, when I am going to work, so this is nothing unusual.

But, what happens next was unusual. I wash up and had almost finished putting my clothes on when I hear a noise at my door. It sounds kind of like a knock. It sounds like three knocks to be exact.

"Knock, knock, knock," it sounds like what I heard.

I was suddenly scared. I wasn't expecting any company this early in the morning. Besides, the screen door was supposed to have been locked, so how can someone knock directly on my apartment door.

The knock startles and frightens me so, that I said aloud, "Oh my goodness. What was that?"

After I said that, my Angel Spirit got my attention.

I heard, "Don't go to work today. If you do, something bad is going to happen."

I was really frightened now. I got so scared untill I didn't know what to do. I didn't want to go outside the apartment, but I didn't want to stay inside the apartment either.

I left. I was moving so fast, that I left my door ajar. I decide to ask Daddy Nathaniel if it was him at the door. I ran out of my apartment to Daddy's apartment and began banging on his door.

"Who is it?" Daddy said.

"It's me," I reply in a panicky voice.

Daddy immediately opens the door and asks in an anxious voice, "Honey, what's wrong?"

"Was that you who came to my door and knocked three times and said something was going to happen to me if I went to work," I blurt out sounding very much out of breath.

"No, baby it wasn't me," Daddy said concerned. "If something told you that then don't you go to work today? I'll give you money when I get home from my job."

"Okay," I said feeling relieved.

I left Daddy's apartment so he can get dress for work. I didn't want to go home yet, so I went over to Ms. Gertrude's apartment. She was usually up, watching out of the window as I went to work.

Ms. Gertrude Miller is her full name. She is much older than me and is from Jacksonville, Florida. I lived in Jacksonville when I was younger, but we didn't know one another then. We became friends in spite of our age difference.

Ms. Gertrude opens the door in her house coat.

"Was that you who knocked three times on my door and told me not to go to work and if I do something was going to happen?" I blurt out sounding out of breath again.

"No, baby it wasn't me," Ms. Gertrude said looking very concerned. "If something told you that, then you stay home," she says beckoning me inside her apartment.

"Come on in, and we'll talk a few minutes," Ms. Gertrude said opening her door wide to let me in.

She then says, "Then later on I'll buy us some beer when the store opens."

I quickly went inside. Ms. Gertrude then asks, "What bus were you going to get on."

"Mr. George Washington's bus," I reply as she closes the door behind us. That is the bus I would ride to the tomato farm.

Ms. Gertrude and I talk with each other for a little while longer. I feel much better about things, so I went back to my apartment.

Suddenly, around two in the afternoon, I can hear Ms. Gertrude yelling from her apartment to mine.

"Frances! Frances come here! Run, run," I heard her yelling.

I quickly ran to her apartment. I didn't know what was wrong. Her door was open, so I entered.

"Look! Look!" Ms. Gertrude said pointing avidly at the TV in her living room.

I can see that the news was on. The news was saying that Mr. George Washington's bus was in an accident. The bus went into the canal and several people lost their lives. People were badly injured.

"Thank you, Jesus! You saved me from death!" I said aloud in a grateful voice.

"Yeah, God saved you!" Ms. Gertrude said happily.

I immediately thought of my Angel Spirit. The Angel had warned me not to go to work today. But, more importantly, I listened to my Angel Spirit. I'm very glad that I listened, because I can't swim a lick. I probably would have drowned in that bus crash.

I don't go back to work for several days after the crash. I didn't go back to the same job because there wasn't a bus to take us there. I was kind of glad I wasn't working on the tomato farm anymore. Now the small allergic bumps on me can begin to clear up.

I continue going to the loading zone seeking employment. Sometimes, I got a job. Sometimes, I didn't. I soon landed another job and I work for several more months.

Although, I was enjoying being around Daddy Nathaniel and living in my own apartment, I was beginning to get home sick for New Jersey. Out of the different places that I have lived, I call New Jersey my home.

A friend of mine was going that way and asks if I want to ride. He was heading to Patterson, New York. Since the trip was on the house, I figure I would ride and be that much closer to home,

New Jersey. So, I pack my bags, said goodbye to Daddy Nathaniel, and left.

By now Momma and Big Momma are living in New Jersey too.

THE MIRACLE OIL

Let us fast forward to the almost present. I presently live in New Jersey in an apartment with my daughter, Princess, and her family. We've been living here for the last five years or so. I used to work right across the street, about forty years ago, taking care of white folks in their homes. Today it's called home health care work. Back then, it was just called work.

In the apartment I am living in, I would often times hear people making noises in the kitchen and bedroom. I can never tell where the voices are coming from though.

Sometimes, there is knocking at the door or the doorbell starts ringing. Yet, when we open the door no one is there.

It was about four years ago, 2017, when all of a sudden, I start seeing white folks coming through the door into the apartment. That scared me a whole lot.

The first time it happens, I am sitting on the couch with my eyes half closed. I open my eyes wide, and I see a white man Spirit come through the door. The door isn't even open. He scares the hell out of me. The white man Spirit walks into the apartment. As he is walking, he disappears right in front of me.

I almost peed on myself. Just like when I almost did while living in that rotten shack with Cousin Sally and Cousin Buddy.

Knock, knock, knock and nobody is there. Ring, ring, ring and no one is there. Those spirits aggravate me so much that I want to move.

One day, I went into the living room. That is where I see a young white woman Spirit with blonde hair coming through the closed door. She stops and began looking at the mail in her hands. She is standing there looking down and shifting through the mail when I move. She turns my way, still holding the mail in her hand, and takes two steps inside the doorway towards me and suddenly disappears.

I continue to hear knocking and doorbells ringing. One Saturday night I was watching TV. There isn't anything on TV that I want to see, so I start flipping the channels. I turn the channel to Daystar TV.

I start to change the channel when my Angel Spirit says, "don't change the channel. Watch this."

So, I start watching the TV show when a man came on by the name of Marcus Lamb. He began to talk about and introduce a friend of his, Prophet Dwight Pate. He said something similar to this.

"I want to introduce you to a friend of mine, Prophet Dwight Pate. I've known him for 30 years. You can depend on his word. He is one of the most powerful Prophets that I know."

He went on to say that Prophet Dwight Pate has brought some powerful oil with him.

The bottle of oil cost a total of four hundred and eighty dollars. Some of the money for the oil went to charity. So, I buy some. I pay four hundred and eighty dollars for that bottle of oil. Once a month, for a whole year, I'd send in forty dollars until I paid the Miracle Oil off.

As soon as I got the oil, I anoint the doors, the windows, and everything else I can think of. That's what helps stop the spirits from coming inside the apartment bothering me so much. It was indeed Miracle Oil for me.

One of my eyes is close to being blind. I sometimes will put a small amount of oil on top of my eyelid and seems like I can see a little better. I put some on a knot on my knee and it doesn't hurt as much anymore. I tell everyone I know about the Miracle Oil and a lot of them bought some too.

... I still use Prophet Pate's (Bishop Pate) Miracle Oil today, only I don't pay for it anymore. It's free. At times, when I am able, I'll give a donation. Prophet Pate sends thousands and maybe even hundreds of thousands of bottles of Miracle Oil to people for free all the time. He has been doing this for a lot of years.

Today, many people call in to give testimony regarding the Miracle Oil on Bishop Pate's prayer line on Tuesday nights at 8:00 p.m. I listen most Tuesday nights myself. I think he is a wonderful blessing and a good man! Just call and ask him for some oil and you got it! …

THE KNOCK ON THE DOOR

I guess you might be wondering how in the world I can see people walking through walls. The earliest I can remember being different, I guess, is when I was three years old living in Florida. I don't really know that I am different; I just know what is.

Momma has a one big room apartment that we are living in. We put two beds in that one big room. There is also a little stove in the middle of the room. The air in the room would often fill up with Momma's good cooking. I like living here. I always like it when we have our own place.

One day, there was a knock on the door.

I can hear Momma say, "Who is it?" Momma never stops cooking as she answers the knock on the door.

Then I hear a man's voice. The man says his name, but I can't remember it. After all, I'm only three years old.

Momma walks toward the door and opens it. The man came inside our apartment.

"Do you want anything today?" he asks Momma.

"No, I don't want nothing today." Momma replies as she began to briskly stir what she was cooking in the pot.

And then it happens; the strangest thing. I saw death on that man as he turns to go out of the door. I try desperately to tell him not to go outside, because a man was going to hurt him.

I began pulling on his hand. I pull on his shirt tail. I pull on his pants leg. I patted his leg. I did everything that I can think of at the age of three to get his attention.

I said, "Missah, Missah! That man! That man! That man!"

When I did get the man's attention and before I can say anything more the man reaches down and pats me on the head and says, "Yeah, baby. Yeah, baby," and walks out the door.

After he went outside, he must have taken about three or four steps, when suddenly a man shoot and kills him. The person who kills the man also robs him. I was sad.

I can hear Momma later talking on the phone to my Aunts and different people.

She said in a matter of fact voice, "Frances tried to warn him. Frances kept pulling on him and pulling on him. She tried to tell him not to go outside, because he was going to die. He didn't listen to Frances. He just patted her on the head and left out the door."

Needless to say, I heard that story repeated quite a few times for a while. I felt a little different from that day on.

I eventually learn that the man who knocked on the door was a number runner. He would play lottery numbers for people in the streets, as it is sometimes called. He came over to see if Momma wanted to play a number. I guess someone saw him, or followed him and wanted to hurt that man.

Momma would play and win most of the time. She just never has a lot of money to put on a number at one time, so she only wins a little money when her number comes out.

… Playing numbers in the street was popular in Florida back then and probably still might be. I don't know any more. I know it was labeled illegal gambling. I'm not living in Florida now, but I can bet that people are still playing numbers in the streets. …

THE SUN HEALED ME

There is another time that I almost forgot about. I'm about nine years old or so. We move back down South from New Jersey. Momma and us kids move into my Uncle's house. He has a four bedroom house on some acres of land. He has the house divided like it was two apartments. My Aunt and Uncle live on one side with two rooms, and we live on one side with two rooms.

Every night we would lie down in the bed. I would start to go to sleep, but then I would hear horses running. The horse's hooves were hitting the ground hard. It sounds like a great stampede as they gallop across my Uncle's land. It scared me so badly.

All the noises kept me from going to sleep at night. After not being able to sleep at night, I soon got sick. I got very sick. Momma didn't have no money to take me to the doctor. Nobody had fifteen cents to get a loaf of bread much less money for a doctor.

This day I was so sick that I didn't know what to do. My head is hot with fever. I go outside on the porch and look up at the Sun. The Sun is burning hot! It is about one hundred degrees, or so, outside it seems.

I feel so weak. I look up at the Sun and say, "Jesus, have mercy on me." I fall to the floor and instantly go to sleep with the hot sun shining down on me. When I woke up, I tell you, I was just like a brand new flower. It was as if I was never sick.

I know God is a healer. My Momma and us kids don't go to the doctor often. We don't have money for a doctor. Momma gives us herbs and she prays a lot. Momma prays an awful lot.

… I believe in my heart that the galloping horses were Spirits that I heard while living on my Uncle's land. Maybe my Uncle's house was built on a slave plantation or Indian land.

I believe whatever happened on that land and along that street was bad. It must have been some really evil things that took place on my Uncle's land before he bought it.

I remember looking down the street out of my Momma's window, and I saw a man without a head standing by the telegraph pole. Yes, I seen that and it scared me so badly when I was a little girl. I was scared to look out the windows for days. That was another reason why I hardly slept while living in my Uncle's house.

My Uncle's wife was supposed to leave that land to us, my Uncle's nieces and nephews, when she died. They never had children and that was my Uncle's wish. She died many years later and had another family.

Needless to say, my Aunt never did leave the land to us, and we never got that land. I don't think that I would ever be able to live there anyway. ...

SANDRA AND THE TOUCH

I am around twenty nine years old, and I am living in this apartment complex. A lady name Sandra lives in the apartment complex also. Sandra has two sisters, and they all are some beautiful tall girls; but Sandra went for bad.

I bought a money order to pay on a bill of mine. A forty dollar money order that I thought was on my dresser in my bedroom, but it's not. I have misplaced my money order. I'm not sure where that money order can be.

I began looking everywhere, everywhere for my money order. I had taken my bag of garbage out to the garbage house earlier, and I thought maybe I put the money order in the garbage by mistake. So, I went back outside to the garbage house to look through my garbage.

Sandra lives upstairs in back of me by the garbage house. The garbage house is a separate building where your garbage is supposed to go. Though, some people just throw their garbage anywhere, I suppose most people throw their garbage away in the garbage house.

My apartment is in the front by the street. There is a street light facing towards my apartment. I am glad there is a street light there. It comes in handy at night.

Since Sandra's apartment is near the garbage house, Sandra sees me going through my garbage looking for my money order. She is in the window looking down at me. She starts calling me all kinds of names.

I said, "Sandra, please leave me alone," and continue looking through my garbage.

Sandra turns to her sister, who is by the window with her, and shouts, "She's scared of me. Look at her. She's scared of me."

I continue to rummage through my garbage. I am hoping I'd find my money order so I can hurry up and leave. Meanwhile, Sandra continues to talk so badly about me.

I'm trying to ignore her, but I said again, "Sandra, please leave me alone," still trying to mind my business.

So, Sandra keeps on calling me all kinds of bad names and I keep begging her to leave me alone. I got so tired of her running her mouth that I decide to forget the money order and just walk away. I turn to go to my apartment.

Sandra came flying down the stairs and starts following me around. As I got to the steps that led to my apartment, Sandra gets on a step so close to me that we touched briefly. I had begged Sandra over and over to leave me alone.

I turn around and said in a had enough voice, "Didn't I tell you to leave me alone," touching Sandra lightly on her leg.

When I touched Sandra, she flew up about five feet in the air. When she came down, I didn't see her. I must have blinked my eyes because Sandra was gone.

Sandra saw me about two weeks later walking down the street. She looks scared. Sandra looks scared of me instead of me scared of her. It's like the shoe is on the other foot.

Sandra says, "Hi, Frances baby."

I say, "Hi Sandra," and laugh lightly.

Sandra says, "Baby, if anybody mess with you, let me know. I'm going to help you beat their a--."

I just laugh again and say, "Okay, Sandra."

I never saw Sandra again after that day. She moves away from over by me. I wondered for years, though, how did I just touch her, and she flew up in the air. I must have had some help from God, or my Angels, because I'm real scary. Besides, I barely touched her.

I remember Sandra had on very tight blue jeans that day. Every time I tried to get a hold of her, I couldn't grab her or her clothing. I guess that's why I was only able to barely touch her leg.

When I did touch Sandra's leg, she went flying high up in the air. For real, I barely touched her. I guess I must have had the Midas touch.

THE MAN AT PENN STATION

My goodness how time flies. It's been a lot of years since I was twenty nine. I still like to pray a lot, and I like to preach to try to uplift someone. I enjoy talking to the homeless telling them that God loves them too. I would some days go to Penn Station, where I know a lot of homeless people are, and I talk to them about God; that Spirit in you.

Pennsylvania Station, better known as Penn Station, is a huge bus and train terminal where around a half a million people commute daily. It is one of the busiest rail and bus terminals in North America. It connects to the New York City Subway Station, New Jersey Transit, the Long Island Railroad, and Amtrak.

Lots and lots of food vendors are located in and around Penn Station. There's the Shake Shack, L'Amico, Friedman's, Keens Steakhouse, Riko Chelsea, Ichiran, just to name a few. Yes, even a McDonald's can be found.

Oh, I almost forgot to mention the Pennsy, a food hall that houses appetites from vegan food, Korean food, and just about every other food. Most any kinds of food you want to eat can be bought in the Pennsy.

I have been going to preach at Penn Station for just about twenty years now. My Spirit told me to go there. The people at Penn Station told me that I can preach outside Penn Station just not inside.

So, I wait until people either come out of Penn Station or I speak to them before they go into Penn Station. I would talk to them about God. I would even get on the bus and speak the Word at times. Most times, I just speak to whoever is around, telling them about the graces of God.

Most people in the streets call me Grandma. I guess I look like a grandma to the young, the old, white people, and everyone else. I don't mind being called Grandma. Helping people is my passion.

There are lots of homeless people who live or hang around Penn Station. They don't have anywhere to go. They even have a jailhouse at Penn Station just for the homeless people; it often seems like, though the jail is for everyone. One day, I would like to build homes for the homeless people. Yes, that's my dream!

One Saturday morning my granddaughter and I went to Penn Station. The weekend brings a lot of people to Penn Station. Today was no exception. There are people everywhere you look. I was in Booth Three with my granddaughter, when the Spirit spoke to me.

The Spirit said, "Say this!"

So, I said in a sudden voice, "It's somebody out here that's sick and sick enough to die; but if you call on Jesus, he'll heal you."

My granddaughter looks at me with raised eyebrows. She has been here with me before, and she knows I preach and talk a lot.

I didn't talk that loudly at first, so I speak louder and turns around in a complete circle as I speak again.

"Somebody out here is sick. Sick enough to drop dead. If you call on Jesus, he will heal you," I shout as loudly as I can.

My granddaughter stood up, and we both went to the next booth, Booth Two. As loudly as I had spoken, seem like the people in Booth Two should have heard me.

God wants to heal that person and I have to do what God wants me to do, so we continue on to the next booth. Anyway, by the time we got to the next booth, Booth Two, a man had fell dead just that quickly.

"Is he dead?" I ask a cop.

The only thing the cop said is, "Were waiting for the people to come get him now."

"Is he dead?" I ask the cop again.

The cop replies in an agitated voice. "I said we're waiting for the people to come get him now." Then the cop turns away.

I move forward to peer at the man. The man was not breathing.

"Ump, ump, ump," I exclaim aloud.

I turn around and gather my belongings and my granddaughter, and I went back to Booth Three. My granddaughter and I soon board our bus back home. It feels good to be going home now. It was a sad day at Penn Station. A sad day indeed!

A WAR IS COMING

I began dreaming in November 2019, the same dream, over and over and over again. In my dream, I am running. Every time I look back, there is this white man in a white sheet running behind me. The man has a lot of blood on the front of the sheet he is wearing. I was really scared. I was so scared and I ran, and I ran as fast as I could, trying to get far away.

When I suddenly awakened from my dream, I began staring into space at nothing in particular, except the white wall next to the dresser in my bedroom. The dream was so real and startling to me that I can only stare and wonder.

I wonder why I am dreaming such a frightening and bloody dream.

Then the Spirit spoke to me and said, "It's going to be a war."

A war I thought. "Lord have mercy. Umph, umph, umph," I said out loud in my bedroom.

I stood up and walk slowly to the window. I look out of the window. It is a beautiful, crisp and sunny day, and doesn't look as if a war is coming. I began to dress as quickly as I can. I have to warn everyone that a war is coming.

As I step outside, I can see people walking normally without a care in the world, except to get wherever they are going. I hop on the bus going to Penn Station. There are lots of people on the bus.

I said, "A war is coming! If you can afford it, you need to stock up on food. If you can buy food, buy can food, dry food, and food that you can put in your freezer. Get it; because there is going to be a shortage of food soon."

The people look at me like I was crazy. Some of them point at me. Some of them talk about me. Some of them whisper about me. Some even grin right in my face about it.

The bus finally makes it to Penn Station. I impatiently wait for the bus door to open. When the door opens, I quickly get off the bus, and I went around and told anyone that would listen.

I shout, "There is going to be a war. Everybody stock up on food because food is going to be scarce. If you can buy food, buy can food, dry food, and food that you can put in your freezer."

I went to bus after bus after bus booths. I was once told that I could preach outside but not inside the building, even though I have a Missionary certificate. I would either get on the bus or wait for people to get off the buses and yell as loudly as I can.

"A war is coming! A war is coming! Everybody stock up on food and water because it's going to be hard to find food and water soon."

I yell again as loudly as I can so that more people can hear me.

"A war is coming! A war is coming! Stock up on food and water! If you can buy food, buy can food, dry food, and food that you can keep in your freezer," I repeat over and over again.

I went into nail salons and different shops to tell the people in there. The people there look at me like that woman needs to go where they put crazy people.

I don't care. I just warn them anyway. They can't say I didn't warn them.

I went into doctor's offices, and I told them that a war is coming. The people there look at me as if they want to say something, but they don't.

I went to blood centers where people donate blood, and I told them about a war is coming.

One lady said, "It ain't going to be no war. Not in the United States. America is not going to have a war," she says in disbelief.

Although everyone has an accent, the lady sounds as if she has roots in another country and can't believe that America will have a war.

"You'll see. You'll see," I said as I went anxiously out of the door to tell others. I went everywhere I knew to speak, where people wouldn't tell me to get out.

I spoke to a preacher who I see at the terminal from time to time.

"Sir, my Angel Spirit told me that there is going to be a war," I mention.

The preacher looks at me and says in a loud, thunderous voice, "God is going to take care of me."

… The preacher testified some months later in the year 2020 that I was right.

He said, "Yeah, you told me to get some food, and I went to Railway Avenue. They didn't hardly have no meat there. Yeah, you told me," he repeated.

Now Railway Avenue is the name of a street in New Jersey. There are a plethora of butcher shops on that street such as: Al Hilal Meat & Fish Market, Paradise Halal Meats, Islam Brother's Halal Live Poultry, Hafez Halal Meat and Grocery, Al Quds Super Market,

Mennella Market Place Fresh Meat, Alhabbak Halal Mini Market, Brothers Produce just to name a few. I hope the businesses survived during the Pandemic of 2020.

If you can't find meat on Railway Avenue then you can bet that there is a shortage! …

You have to pay attention to your dreams. It means something when you dream. Like if you are laughing with a dead person in your dream then it usually means that you will be crying about something after a while.

If I dream about meat, more often than not, it means that someone I know will have an operation soon. Sometimes the operation is successful and sometimes it is not. Other times after I dream about meat, someone I know gets sick and may not have an operation. I just don't like to dream about meat, but sometimes I do.

I was once told that young people have visions, and old people have dreams. I feel that dreams and visions have meaning and are trying to tell you something. You have to watch your dreams. If you forget that you dreamed a dream, then it doesn't mean much. If you remember the dream, it can mean a whole, whole lot of things.

You just have to pay attention to your dreams. If something bad happens, then you know that's probably what your dream was about, because it will come out. More often than not something in that dream will come to pass. Pay attention.

THE PANDEMIC

A few months later, around March of 2020, Coronavirus came to be known in the United States of America. Though there were reports of people being ill in the United States months before now. The Government, at that time, thought that basically the

Coronavirus is nothing to worry about and would disappear soon. Well, disappear it didn't.

It seems the Coronavirus was affecting people in other parts of the world too like; Wuhan, China. Actually, according to W.H.O., The World Health Organization, in December 2019, Wuhan China began treating dozens of cases of an unknown pneumonia. China's first death was reported on January 11, 2020. It was a sixty one year old man.

The same type of illness was soon reported in other countries like Japan, South Korea, and Thailand in January 2020. The first confirmed case in the United States came the next day in

Washington State according to The World Health Organization. A man in his thirties developed symptoms after returning from a trip to Wuhan, China.

Because the Coronavirus, also known as Covid 19, is affecting people all over the globe, it's labeled as a Pandemic. Travel was soon banned to other parts of the World as a new reality began to set in. I like to travel, but suddenly, I was afraid to travel.

It suddenly dawns on me that this is the war that I was warned about in my dreams. I quickly call my Aunt and tell her.

My Aunt said, "I know baby, I know baby," before we said goodbye.

I remember when Covid 19 first was known in the United States; it seems as if I had all of the symptoms. I got the dry cough. I got the fever. I got the chills. I lost my sense of smell. I lost my sense of taste. I also got a light headache.

I quickly call to my two little granddaughters. One is four and the other is ten years old.

"I'm going to anoint your hands," I said while gently spreading Miracle Oil on both of their hands. I then swiftly anoint my head with the oil too.

After anointing my head and their hands generously with the Miracle Oil, I said to my two granddaughters.

"I want you to put your hands on me and repeat what I say."

They did exactly what I said. I told one granddaughter to put her hand in my chest, and I told the other granddaughter to put her hand on my back. I then asked them to say what I say.

"In the name of Jesus, stain of death, go back to where you came from in the pits of hell," I said with authority!

They repeat what I said and my symptoms rapidly disappear. I felt that stain of death lifting off me and leaving my body. I felt well again. My granddaughters can testify to this. I soon got a Covid test, but it did not detect any Covid. I am thankful for that.

Meanwhile, people began dying left and right in the United States and worldwide from Covid 19. Some people are here today and gone tomorrow. That's just how fast some people are dying from this virus.

From watching the news on T.V., at first, the Coronavirus appears to affect the elderly the most. Nursing Homes are hit hard and visitors are soon banned from visiting loved ones, which results in more and more elderly people dying alone.

The public is not allowed to enter nursing homes anymore. Family and loved ones sometimes would visit their family by standing outside their window and holding up signs. They celebrated birthdays and anniversaries outside of the windows at the Nursing Home.

I used to work taking care of the elderly, and I tell you, I have never seen nothing like this before. Imagine not being able to visit your elderly grandparents, your parents, your sons, and daughters, or your loved ones at nursing homes. Unimaginable, but it's happening now.

Some states call on the National Guard to assist at nursing homes. The National guards assist with sanitizing the nursing homes by wiping down computers, and desks, mopping floors, relieving overworked staff, assisting with removing the dead, and helping out wherever needed. Thank God for the National Guards.

Hospitals began to fill up with Covid patients. We are hit especially hard in New Jersey where the death count is high.

Makeshift hospitals are set up by the National Guards either in the hospital parking lots or in a separate building. So many people are getting sick and dying that the hospitals and ambulances can't keep up. Dead bodies are stacking up and have to sit for days in refrigerated trucks or makeshift morgues. Even the funeral homes are backlogged.

The news said at first that only the elderly and people with compromised health conditions are affected by Covid 19. But soon, younger and younger people became ill and died. People in their sixties, fifties, forties, thirties, twenties, and maybe younger began to die from this deadly disease. Age didn't seem to matter anymore. It was just a number. This Virus was beginning to affect everyone.

I continue to pray for the world. Lord help us all. Actually, I pray an awful lot. I sometimes pray three and four times a day. I pray long deep prayers. I also pray short prayers at times.

Sometimes, I pray for hours and hours like my Momma used to pray.

I was praying one day, and the Spirit spoke to me and said, "None of your Aunt Jenny's children have died in a long time," the Spirit said in a matter-of-fact voice.

It has been a long time since my cousin passed, Aunt Jenny's daughter. It's been almost twenty years ago.

I grab the phone and called an Aunt of mine. After my Aunt answered, I said, "The Spirit spoke to me about Aunt Jenny's kids. The Spirit said that none of her children have died in a long time," I tell my Aunt."

It was about two weeks later when that same Aunt whom I told about my dream called me.

She says, "You know your Cousin Carlton died."

Since I have two cousins named Carlton, I quickly asked my Aunt, "Which Cousin Carlton died?" Uneasily awaiting her answer, I found myself holding my breath.

Auntie said, "Your Aunt Jenny's son."

"That's what the Spirit told me," I said to my Aunt.

My Aunt exclaims, "Yeah, I know. I remember what you told me."

That's when my Aunt starts saying that I was a Prophet. The Spirit doesn't say that I am a Prophet. The Spirit told me that if I open my mouth, he would speak through me. I do believe that my Mom was a Prophet, though. Momma dreamed of things that happened. May she rest in peace!

I sure hate to hear about Cousin Carlton's passing. After Cousin Carlton dies, his sister soon dies too. I'm not sure if their deaths are Covid 19 related or not. I didn't make it to the funerals because of the Coronavirus war, but I surely included the family in uplifting prayers.

THE PANDEMIC SURGES

At first, I thought I heard on the news that The World Health Organization and the CDC, which is The U.S. Centers for Disease Control and Prevention say that the Virus is not airborne. Then I thought I heard on the news that the Virus is airborne. I guess no one really knows much about this virus. It's hard to know what to believe, much less who to believe. But we got to believe in something.

Schools are the first to close down. In-person schools in my area closed for over a year. I look after my granddaughters while they attend school virtually. Students began to learn virtually as people continue to die from Covid 19. Yes, imagine that, online schooling.

People keep dying. Billions of people are asked to wear masks and face shields in public and at home. At first, when I went to the grocery stores some people had on masks, and some people did not wear masks. Eventually, most stores post signs that masks must be worn inside of the store.

People stand in line for hours at a time waiting to purchase food and other items such as paper towels, toilet paper, sanitizing wipes, rubbing alcohol, Lysol, and even baby diapers just to name a few, only to finally get inside and find empty shelves. Empty shelves were everywhere.

Just about the only businesses that are allowed to stay open are grocery stores and gas stations. Grocery stores like Aldi, BJ's, Key Foods, Save A Lot, Stop and Shop, Acme, Weis Markets, Wegmans and many others start closing earlier than normal.

Although Kroger is one of the nation's largest grocery store chains, none is located in New Jersey. My friend has a Kroger where she lives in Georgia, and the Kroger stores are closing early there too.

In some places, the lines are wrapped around the parking lot. The CDC recommends people to social distance themselves at least six feet from each other to help stop the spread of the Coronavirus. Some people distance themselves and some people don't.

Soon just about all businesses are posting that masks must be worn. A lot of states and cities even make masks mandatory in public, but not all states and cities make masks mandatory. The infection rate kept going up!

Businesses shut down for months and months at a time. Businesses like gyms, salon parlors, and bars, completely close down for many months. Some people still went to salon parlors and bars, and the infection rate kept going up!

Some Government agencies and banks are not open to the public. A lot of Government agencies only do business via mail or email or online. They don't open their doors to the public.

A lot of banks only conduct in-person business via the drive-thru window. Long lines began to form. Some people are patient, and some people are not patient.

Yes, even churches start closing down too, because infection rates are so high. This angers some people and services are still held and many people gather. The infection rate kept going up! A lot of people got infected at church according to the news. I guess if it was a small church that would be a whole lot of the congregation.

Later on churches start having drive-in church services. Just like at a drive-in movie. People would park and stay in their vehicles and listen to the Preacher preach. Can you imagine that?

Most of the restaurants close and people quickly went to ordering online, or calling in their orders for delivery or pick up. Sometimes delivery is free, but most times it's not. Delivery is big business now, especially, in America. If you want to order out you can have it delivered, or you can pick up your purchase in the drive-thru window.

A lot of businesses, if they don't have a drive-thru window, created one. Some business owners literally cut a hole in their wall just to serve people, trying to stay in business. Some simply open their door and place your order outside. Some businesses survive the Covid 19

Pandemic; some businesses don't survive the Covid 19 Pandemic.

Thousands of people lose their jobs. People are ill with Covid 19. Businesses that are still open are operating with fewer people. Fewer people at work mean less production. That's how product shortages came about according to the news.

Food became harder to get and took a while to reach store shelves. It became harder to find meat, water, milk, and many other products.

Products like bathroom tissue, paper towels, and even masks are hard to find. Hospitals are running out of N95 masks and other medical supplies.

Doctors, nurses, and staff began reusing masks according to the news.

The Federal Government soon mandates the making of masks a high priority. Certain businesses stop making their usual products to make more masks. Other businesses volunteer to assist.

These are indeed trying times. Curfews became active in many states, including New Jersey. My friend in Georgia says that people have to be off the streets by 9:00 p.m. unless they are going to work or have a legitimate reason for being out.

That doesn't seem to stop people. People still find a way to congregate and hospitals continue to fill up with Covid

19 patients. People wait in line and sometimes for days, for a hospital bed or ventilator.

Thousands of people got infected in New Jersey. A lot of people are dying. Most people die alone in hospitals or nursing homes because patients can't have visitors for fear of the virus spreading. Many people die at home also.

A new era indeed! I never thought that I would see such at my age, and I'm in my seventies now. I don't think life will ever be the same again. It will always be different now.

The Virus continues to devastate people all around the world. According to health organizations, The United States surpassed 20 million infections from Covid 19 and more than 300,000 deaths by December 31, 2020.

Many people all over the world are losing their lives to the Coronavirus disease. New Jersey Covid 19 deaths are reported to be over 26,000 according to the news.

That is a lot of lives lost. Fathers, Mothers, Sons, Daughters, Sisters, Brothers, Nieces, Nephews, Cousins, Friends, and Co-Workers have all died from this devastating virus and still are dying. I even lost family and friends to this disease.

Eventually, vaccines became available. In the spring of 2021, it seems as if the Coronavirus was beginning to finally get under control. Less people became infected and less people are dying. The CDC now recommends that vaccinated people don't have to wear masks around other vaccinated people or in most public places.

The masks came off. Restaurants no longer have social distancing restrictions and people can come inside and eat. Bars reopen. Concerts began to happen and all you need to be is vaccinated.

At some point, the CDC recommendation changes to three feet apart instead of six feet. I hope the infection rate doesn't rise again.

I like to go by the CDC's first social distance recommendation. I try to stand six feet apart when I am at the grocery store if I don't forget. I carry alcohol wipes too.

The infection rate went back up! Covid 19 cases began to surge. A new variant of the Virus emerges name Delta, and people start getting sick again including vaccinated people. Hospitals once again are filling up with unvaccinated people according to the news. The CDC now recommends that everyone wear masks including vaccinated people.

I don't go to Penn Station anymore to preach to the homeless. I haven't been since the Pandemic hit in early 2020. I bet there are even more homeless people than before at Penn Station.

I find myself still praying a lot nowadays. I even fast at times when I am praying hard. I still believe that prayer brings about change.

Lord, help us all. I didn't expect this kind of war, but I'm glad that I was able to survive it thus far, and I was able to warn some people.

Everyone has that Spirit inside and is surrounded by Angels. Angels to help guide, comfort, and direct you along your journeys. Anyone can ask for their Angels' help. Yes, anyone can.

You have to pay attention to your dreams, believe them or not. Above all, listen to what your Spirit tells you. I did and I'll always be grateful for what The Angels Told Me.

CONTACT

AngelSpiritBooks@yahoo.com

Angel Spirit Books

P. O. Box 2194

Stone Mountain, GA 30086

REFERENCES

Centers for Disease Control and Prevention, C. D. C: Coronavirus Pandemic; Information and Protocols; U. S. Deaths; Covid 19 Cases. 2020 – 2021

Mary B. Frances: recalling her life story. 1944 – 2021 ...

Mary B. Frances and A. Z. Love: Coronavirus Pandemic; Information both authors witnessed and are living through in the States that they reside. 2020 – 2021

World Health Organization, W. H. O: Coronavirus Pandemic; Information and Protocols; U. S. Deaths; Covid 19 Cases. 2020 – 2021

ACKNOWLEDGMENTS

First and foremost, all praises are due to The Almighty for giving me the strength and voice to write this book. Thank you, **Almighty**!

Thank you, Family, for believing the best and showing patience on this most gracious journey. Thank you, **Family**!

Special thanks to you, **Amber, Angel, Bonnie, and Bonnie's Mom, Dorothea, Jeffery, Patricia, Regina, Sharon, Shay, Wanda,** and everyone who has been instrumental in helping to bring this book to life with your encouragement and feedback. Thank you, **Everyone**!

Last but not least! Many thanks and blessings to all of you remarkable Readers out there for supporting this book. Thank you, awesome **Readers**!

Peace n Grace ...

ANGEL SPIRIT BOOKS

AngelSpiritBooks@yahoo.com

WHAT KIND OF PRAYERS

What kind of prayers do you pray
Prayers of wants or prayers of faith
Prayers of mercy, prayers of greed
Prayers of spite or prayers of need

Whatever prayer you do say
Be very careful of what you pray
You never know what's in store
You may just get what you pray for

So, pray for the will to do all good things
The courage to face what each day brings
The sense to know right from wrong
The strength to always carry on

The art of giving, the joy of living
And most of all and every day
Be very thankful when you pray
For this is one way to receive grace
To always, always give praise

— Journey of Thoughts, 1997

ABOUT THE AUTHOR

This is the first book by Mary B. Frances and A. Z. Love. Before the Covid 19 Pandemic of 2020, Mary would enjoy uplifting the hopeless and homeless through caring words of encouragement and prayer while doing Missionary work. She still prays often and aspires to one day provide shelter for the homeless. That is her first passion.

Mary B. Frances is retired and lives in New Jersey with her daughter, Princess, and her family. She likes to spend lots of time with her grandchildren. Mary has discovered another passion, writing, and anxiously anticipates the completion of her next book.

A. Z. Love lives in Georgia. She currently works as a secretary in a middle school but enjoys writing. Writing is her passion. She has written several poetry books and is working on a children's book, **My Doggone Family**. A. Z. Love hopes that her writing is fun to read, as well as inspiring.